Unending Grace

NICHELLE LAWRENCE

Printed in the United States of America
Book Coach: Michelle Collins MCOLLINS Enterprise
Photographer: Lizander Cabrera

Lawrence, Nichelle
ISBN: 979-8-218-53988-7

REFLECTIONS ON GRIEF

When you get married at twenty-one, you dream of a future full of adventures, kids, and great success. You never imagine being twenty-five dealing with a cancer diagnosis, doctors, insurance, or even worse, turning twenty-six dealing with funeral homes, ashes, and planning a memorial.

That was exactly where I found myself. Alone with a million and one questions for God. See, I never blamed God for the death of my husband, but I was left with a lot of confusion. I knew that it is God's will to heal every time and I knew that every name, including cancer, has to bow to the Name of Jesus.

There I was in a place where my knowledge and my experience did not match up. God had provided my husband's healing on the cross so I couldn't blame Him and it didn't feel right blaming my husband after all he didn't choose to suffer through cancer and die. So, here is the part where I bought into the lie that if I was a better Christian, if only I would have prayed more, believed harder, memorized and quoted more scriptures, and just had more faith then maybe we would have seen the healing we were believing for.

Guilt and shame moved in and began to consume my thoughts. Then the depression set in and the anxiety attacks started taking over. My husband was gone and with him died the future we had planned.

A couple of weeks after the memorial service, the anxiety attacks and depression were only getting worse. One night I found myself laying in my bed at about 2am unable to sleep crying in a dark room. The only thought in my head was what now?

In that moment I heard God speak to me, he said, *"Lindsey, this may have come as a surprise to you, but do you think this took me by surprise? The future you had planned may have changed but my plans for you are still the same. I still have more in store for you, but you have to decide; you can either lay down and let your future die with your husband or you can stand up and live for me. The choice is yours."*

Before I even knew what I was doing, I jumped out of bed and standing there in my dark room at two in the morning, I began laughing for the first time in a long time. I wish I could say it all instantly got better from there and that the anxiety attacks, shame, and depression all left, but that wouldn't be the truth.

The journey through grief had just begun. The change that night happened in my heart. God had brought hope to my hopeless situation. I realized that the future God had for me could never be stolen, even by death. The book he wrote about my life had not changed. Grief was no longer controlling me; the promises of God had taken over my future.

While grief is important to walk through, it is not a place to get stuck. You still have a great future ahead of you. Grab on to Jesus and allow Him to lead you through to the other side.

Lindsey Causer
Pastor, Mentor, Theologian

Loss is inevitable. It happens every day and all times of the day, in different places in the world. Coping with the loss of someone you love is one of the biggest challenges you'll face. The pain can sometimes feel like it's just too much. I would know because I've suffered plenty of loss in my life, but losing my brother was a tough one for me.

It had been about 4 years since my brother's life was taken and I had just sent every letter that my brother had sent to him while he was in jail. The person who had them felt that I should have them instead. I was only going through and reading my letters when I came across a small paper that read, "*Here is a picture I thought you would like. You're my brother, my best friend, and I need you here to walk me down the aisle.*" I immediately shut down. I was instantly sad and in tears. It broke my heart at that very moment when I realized that what I wrote would never happen! I will never get that moment to have with him to tell him one day *"Don't worry, I found the one. You can let me go."*

Reading my letters brought back so many memories. I was right back to being sad and almost even angry, angry at the fact that I would never get to have that.

It brought back so many more emotions I thought I had worked through. I felt hurt. I felt guilty that my brother was gone because of words I had spoken over him while he was in jail. I found myself holding on to those letters to have comfort. I never knew that the letters would soon become an idol. I sought comfort in the writing and words of my brother when Jesus wanted to be my true comforter in that season of grief I was still very much in.

I'll never forget the encounter and the revelation I had that Jesus didn't bring death, especially a cruel one. He brought life and love so I couldn't even blame Him and He reminded me I couldn't blame myself.

In so many ways He was there with me through every sleepless night and every painful cry I had. He is close to the broken hearted. He heals them and bandages their wounds, but we have to let Him. I had to surrender the hurt in order to allow Him to comfort me. He never left me and sometimes it feels like it'll never get better but with Jesus it becomes bearable. It becomes my testimony to help someone else.

Ashley Delaney
Cosmetologist, Prayer Minister, Administrator

Dedicated to my dad,
who held onto God's unchanging hand
and reminded me that grief is not the end.
I love you.

CONTENTS

Foreword

Much like overcoming a lie or an attack from the enemy, understanding our identity in Jesus Christ as we face grief can change our journey through this season. Many people find themselves in deep sorrow, at loss, or in isolation, but with Jesus, we can still experience hope and strength even through these painful moments. Nichelle Lawrence has done an outstanding job in her book, *Unending Grace,* of communicating effortlessly and understandably through personal experience how to tackle grief through the word of God. Throughout Unending Grace, Nichelle pinpoints common traits for stages of grief, provides powerful scriptures, and equips you with written prayers to declare truth over your life.

Over time I have studied grief through my expertise in psychology and counseling. I have learned that grief is a natural human process that can be crafted differently for everyone who experiences it. There is not a one-size-fits-all remedy because every person processes grief differently and everyone has a different story to share about their loved one. I have studied many theories that tell a person how to deal with grief or the "right" way to cope with a loss of mourning.

I have noticed time and time again the imprisonment and comparison that arises when those who are mourning do not live up to the expectations or timelines of these theories. As I sit in class and listen to the research behind all of this, all I could think about is, if they only knew Jesus! If they only knew Jesus they wouldn't find comfort in false trends, social discourses, and traditional ways the world teaches us on how to deal with a loss.

Theories and remedies continue to be created that produce temporary or false comfort, but there is Jesus who is the ultimate Comforter through the power of the Holy Spirit. Furthermore, one key point that has been mentioned repeatedly throughout my educational journey is how we have been designed to be social creatures who are called to be in relationship with others. Sounds familiar? God designed us to be in close communion with others and even those with fancy titles agree! We have been created to do life with others which is why the enemy's first attack on those who experience hardship is isolation. The enemy begins to remove us away from a place of relationship from the community (the church), from our covering (discipleship), and the Holy Spirit (our Comforter).

The Bible teaches us about the power and anointing in agreement, and the power when two or more are gathered in the name of Jesus. The Bible also instructs us to be transformed by the renewal of our mind and as we defeat the battle of grief, we must overcome the ideas and comforts of this world when it comes to grieving and mourning. We have the power and authority to create our agency on how we respond, where we stand, and what we choose to believe in during these times. We can choose to not conform to the patterns of this world, we can choose Jesus.

I am the first to applaud Nichelle Lawrence for her courage and tenacity in writing Unending Grace. I have had the honor to be a close friend and also serve alongside Nichelle in our church's prayer ministry for over 2 years. I am filled with joy to see Nichelle's heart and character being mirrored throughout Unending Grace as she shows us how she persistently fights for the truth and always runs back to God. This book is more than just a book but allows us to dive into Nichelle's heart for her family and her mending relationship with Jesus, her heavenly Father. It is a personal testimony, where Nichelle walks through the raw and exposed experience of grief through the life of her beautiful mother.

She openly shares her story and how she experienced each stage of grief with her family members. Unending Grace takes you on a voyage where one can hop in and join Nichelle in her story of healing as she continually trusts the Lord by applying truth to every trial she faces. She shows us how to bring the kingdom of heaven down to earth through prayer, faith, and community.

Through written prayers Nichelle walks any believer or non-believer through the process of trusting God through this season as we pull down mental strongholds of lies; She walks us through practical ways to overcome each stage of grief. I highly recommend *Unending Grace* to every person who has experienced grief, is experiencing grief, or wants to learn more about how to understand those who are battling grief.

~ Fernanda Villa
Altar Leader, The Way World Outreach, San Bernardino, California;
Bachelor of Science in Psychology, California State University San Bernardino, California;
Master of Science in Counseling, California State University, San Bernardino, California

Introduction

I was a firm believer in one thing, and that was to be available whenever my mom called. Growing up I knew that my mom was sick, she was a type one juvenile diabetic. Not that I really knew what that meant as a child, until one day she had an insulin reaction. An insulin reaction is something that happens when too much insulin is administered and the sugar levels drop far below what is safe.

I remember on occasion seeing this happen to my mom and it was like she was no longer herself. My mom would get angry in these moments, she would seem erratic, but most of all she would always forget my name. So as a gauge for these events I learned to recognize the change in her eyes and her behavior, and I would say, *"Mom, what's my name?"* To which she would always reply, *"I don't know"*, in a way that still breaks my heart to this day.

So, as I got older, and went off to college and started to experience long courses of time away from my mom, I began to build up this fear. I always had one rule, be available whenever my mom called, whether this meant leaving class, stepping out of work, or stopping a conversation mid-sentence. I had to be there for her.

One day while at work, I broke that rule and my life was never the same. At the time I was an in-home therapist and I was seeing a client whose mom was less than nice and made my skin crawl at the thought of her hovering over every single thing I did. So, I left my phone in my bag.

About thirty minutes into the session, I noticed my phone vibrating in my bag but I tried to stay focused on the session. I let another fifteen minutes go by and it starts ringing again. On the third ring I decided to check it. I had two missed calls from my mom and one from my sister, and the fear and panic set in. I immediately call my mom back and she is not answering. As I begin pacing the floor I call her again, no answer. In the midst of that, my phone starts ringing and it's my sister. *"What's going on?!"*, I exclaimed into the phone. *"Necce, mom had a heart attack"*, she yells into the phone. *"Where are you?"*, she says.

I scramble to grab my belongings as I tell my sister, *"Calm down, tell me what happened, I'm on my way, WHAT HOSPITAL IS SHE AT?"* Full of fear I didn't even remember my shoes as I tried to communicate to my client's mother that my mom, the only person that I ever cared about, was to my knowledge, dying.

"I need to leave, they are taking my mom to the hospital, she's having a heart attack", I say as tears fill my eyes. *"I'm so sorry, I have to go"*, I yell running out the door. *"Your shoes"*, she exclaims. The worst part is I could see how angry she was. Angry that I had to leave, to go see about my best friend.

As I'm getting into the car I get a phone call from my mom. *"Mommy, are you okay? What's going on?"*, I cry. My mom begins to explain to me that she went to Kaiser and they said that her cardiac enzymes were in the range that indicated a heart attack. For some backstory, a few days earlier right before Thanksgiving my mom mentioned to me that she had been feeling pain in her right arm, to which I said you should go to Kaiser because in women it could have something to do with your heart.

Finally, I pull up to St. Mary's Hospital and demand to see my mom. I told them that she was brought in on an ambulance from Kaiser and I needed to see her immediately. The paramedic comes out who had just brought my mom in and says, *"Yes, I can take you right to her"*. My mom was still in the hallway on the stretcher but she smiled and said, *"Baby, you made it."* Then she told me she needed to go to the bathroom. I laughed and told her that I would help her.

As we walked to the bathroom my mom was so full of life joking about the handsome paramedic who helped us and my singleness. I was just happy she seemed like herself.

For the next two days my mom stayed at St. Mary's while they ran a battery of tests, while she waited to be transferred to Kaiser. After determining that she was stable enough for transport on day three she was transferred to Kaiser, Fontana. I ran home and gathered her up some things and myself, and my siblings who wanted to come as well. I hadn't left her side until that moment. That night, a Thursday night my dad had to take my brother to a game and so the rest of us stayed with my mom. I remember her nurse being an awful human and eventually asking us to leave because my mom's IV kept bleeding and I reported her, and said we wanted a new nurse. As you can imagine, the nurse did not like this, but that was my mom.

After heading home that night my dad went back to be with my mom and suggested that I go back to work the next day, and since it was Friday I could come right back after work. I couldn't focus that day at work and I told the teacher in the classroom I was seeing my client in that I would likely have to leave if anything came up.

After lunch I got a phone call from my dad telling me that the test they did on my mom revealed that she had an 89% blockage in her heart. What this meant was that three of the four main arteries or parts of the heart were blocked. I suddenly felt very sick and asked the teacher if I could leave because I needed to be with my mom. When I arrived at the hospital I was informed that they would be doing surgery on her but that she would need to wait until Monday morning when the surgeon came in.

It was now Sunday morning around 5 am. I received a phone call from my dad crying on the phone. I remember my heart dropping because I had only ever heard my dad cry once in my whole life, and it was when his brother died. I instantly recognized the familiar sound. *"Dad what's happening? Calm down dad"*, I said into the phone. For some reason I couldn't cry, I knew this was the moment my life was about to change. I knew that this was the moment I would have to carry my family through as the oldest. I still had siblings who were in high school for crying out loud.

"I think we lost mom", my dad yelled and cried into the phone, barely able to catch his breath. *"Dad, it's okay, it's okay, just breathe, I'm on my way. DO YOU HEAR ME DAD? I'm on my way."* I yelled into the phone. I'll never forget the whimper of pain that came from his voice, *"Okay"*, he said.

I ran downstairs quickly to wake up my family. The first person I saw was my cousin *"Melah, my mom is dead"* I said as I watched her drop to her knees. I continued down the stairs to my siblings. I banged on the door and as it opened *"Mom is dead"*, I said as they began to scream and wail. Suddenly my little brother emerges from the room and runs into the kitchen as I'm holding my sisters assuring them that everything will be alright.

My brother, sixteen years old, grabs a knife from the drawer and aims it at his chest. *"Nooooooo, I don't want to be alive without her"* he screams. I yell for my cousin, an older man to grab him but his face is frozen in fear and shock. *"Lydia"*, I yell my sisters name as she reads my face and we both dart into action. My sister wraps her arms around him and I dislodge the knife from his hands. *"Jimmy, no. Mom wouldn't want this."* I say, still holding back the pain.

Once we gathered our things we headed over to the hospital where I entered the ICU filled with family and friends as I watch the doctors performing chest compressions on my mother. I stood there in silence clutching my siblings' hands. The doctor comes out and begins to pray with us. He literally took our hands and started to pray. I couldn't believe it.

They kept pumping her chest, we stood there for what felt like forever. I then was hit with this sudden peace and knowing that she was gone, so I left. As I stood outside smoking a cigarette with my sister and uncle, at the time I was still teetering with my salvation, I waited for the phone call to confirm what I already knew in my heart. My mom died Sunday, December 4th, 2016; she was 59 years old.

1

What is Loss?

Loss occurs when we lose someone or something that usually triggers a grieving process. It's very easy to hear loss and only consider the death of someone but there are many other ways in which someone can experience loss. I want to share some of those ways before we get into my story. In this instance I will be sharing about the loss of a person, however I do truly believe that God can show up in any form of loss. Since loss triggers a grieving process, I believe that reading this book which walks you through the stages of grief will be of benefit to you, no matter which category of loss you find yourself in right now.

Let's explore a few different types of loss:

1. **Death of a loved one** - this can be a family member, friends, even pets. I've often seen some people grow close enough to their animals that this loss causes the same grief as if it were a family member.

2. **Ambiguous loss** - this type of loss is a loss that has no closure. This can be loss such as a missing person, soldiers missing in action,

those who may be physically present but psychologically absent, such as someone with Alzheimer's or dementia.

3. **Loss of a relationship or Divorce** - the end of a significant relationship.

4. **Loss of a home, job, or financial security.**

5. **Loss of possessions** - this can happen through disasters such as fires or robbery, even misplacing something of significance.

6. **Loss of identity** - sometimes there are significant life events or traumas such as rape that can shift the way someone perceives themselves.

7. **Loss of independence** - through things like ageing, sickness, or disabilities one may lose the ability to care for themselves on their own.

8. **Loss of health** - experiencing a decline in physical or mental health.

I am certain that people experience loss in many different ways outside of what is on this list. Maybe what you're experiencing wasn't listed here but no matter what kind of loss you experience, the process of grief is the same. God is concerned about your loss. When we lose something or someone it always brings some kind of shift in our life. In loss we have to relearn to live without that person, that job, or that security. God desires for us to live full, beautiful lives of abundance, but that life will not be without trials, and it will not be without loss. I believe that in every loss we experience God wants to be there, and I hope by the time you finish this book you realize that even in your hardest moment He was there all along and has a plan.

"A thief has only one thing in mind—he wants to steal, slaughter, and destroy. But I have come to give you everything in abundance, more than you expect — life in its fullness until you overflow!" John 10:10 TPT

2

Shock & Denial

I don't think that there has ever been a situation of loss that shock did not follow. Death is one of those things that no matter how prepared one can be, you're never truly prepared. The Oxford dictionary defines shock as a sudden upsetting or surprising event or experience. This definition is seemingly what we all experience when loss takes us by surprise. However, I want to share with you another definition in the Oxford dictionary. Shock is also defined as a violent shaking movement caused by an impact, explosion, or tremor.

Have you ever noticed how a powerful earthquake tends to throw us off balance? Well, if you've never experienced a strong earthquake, sometimes after it you can feel a little off balance. Imagine this, your entire world just shook and if you weren't prepared for it, you can imagine, you may be a little off balance.

That morning when my dad called I remember feeling like the entire world just shook, and the shock wave that followed hit everyone. The shock that I felt that morning was tangible, more than just a deep disturbance taking over.

It was a living, breathing, physical encounter with something I had never experienced. This was something I could have never prepared myself for.

What happens next? I silently thought to myself as we drove to the hospital. The silence that filled the car was overwhelming. While the thoughts of what to expect plagued me, I also couldn't stop wondering what was going to happen to my family. The image of my brother attempting to end his life kept running through my head.

Okay, first I'll get Jimmy checked in with behavioral health, was one of those thoughts. We pulled into the parking lot of Kaiser Permanente Hospital and I told my siblings I was going to run and get Jimmy checked in and then we could head over to my mom. The nurse in behavioral health greeted us and asked what was going on. *"My brother just tried to kill himself. My mom is here and she may be dead"*, I said, essentially handing him over to her. *"Is it okay if we leave him here while we go meet my dad?"* I asked. She eagerly agreed and assured us that he would be just fine. *"We will be right back for you Jimmy"*, I told him. Something I want to mention is that while all of this was happening, I had made a phone call to my old pastor in Virginia and started to fill her in with what was going on.

Though I was still teetering with my faith, I still knew she knew how to get a prayer through. *"I am about to go into service, but I want you to stay on the phone"*, she reassured me. This wasn't a very big church, it was a small family church of no more than twenty or so people, and they all knew me well.

The pastor started off the service by saying, *"Brothers and sisters, I am on the phone right now with Sister Nichelle"*. She went on explaining the current circumstance and the entire church started to stand in belief that my mom would be alright. So, while I'm dropping off my brother, they go into praise and worship. *"Just praise Him, baby"*, she says. I knew in that moment that she wanted me to recognize that no matter what happened, God is still good.

As I turn the corner and walk through the double doors where my mom's room is, she isn't actually in the room but my dad is standing there seeming a little confused. *"Dad, where's mom?"* I said in a distressed tone. *"She got a pulse"*, he said, tears filling his eyes as he gathered things from the room. I hear the cheers and the praise coming through the phone as I yell, "SHE GOT A PULSE, HALLELUJAH". I started to pray in the spirit, which I hadn't done in what felt like years, certainly not since I started to walk a compromised life.

The spirit of God continued to well up in me, it was almost as if I couldn't stop. For a moment, in this moment, when I felt faith rise up in me, for just a moment the ground stopped shaking. I remember thinking about the goodness of God and how even after everything I had done, He was still going to save my mom.

Fast forward to us standing in that cold hospital hallway with thousands of eyes on us as my family screamed out in pain, suddenly, the ground began to shake again. Almost as quickly as the ground began to shake I felt another wave washing over me, this feeling was unfamiliar. *I have to get my family through this,* I thought to myself. By this time, I had no choice but to come to grips with what God had just done and start to focus on my family. Looking back at it now I realize that the unrecognizable feeling was denial.

The American Psychological Association Dictionary of Psychology defines denial as a defense mechanism in which unpleasant thoughts, feelings, wishes, or events are ignored or excluded from conscious awareness. I thought that I was surrendering to God and accepting His will, accepting what He had done. It was easier to cling to the thought that I was accepting what God wanted and to move on and get my family through this than to admit I was angry.

I always thought that denial meant pretending that something didn't happen, but I knew it happened, it was just something that I simply could not deal with. I chose to be completely aware of what was taking place while simultaneously ignoring the fact that I felt anything at all. I remember plunging so deeply into that denial by trying to logically piece together my next step. I slowly entered the hospital room where my mother lay and I heard her laugh resounding in my thoughts.

"She's laughing", I said, as I touched her feet. I wanted to remember her as an "is", and not a "was". In fact, I refused. I stood there looking at my mom trying to remember her even more alive than she was before she passed. I turned around to see my dad. He nodded his head with a fading smile as the tears fell from his eyes. It's interesting, out of all the details I recall I remember looking at my father and it's like the entire moment washed over me. I wanted to leave the room and move on to the next thing.

As people flooded the room to console my dad, I briefly mentioned to him that Jimmy was in the waiting area of the mental health department waiting to be seen. I exited the room to go see him as my dad started to make phone calls. When I met back up with Jimmy, he was still waiting to be seen and I told him that everything would be okay, and that I would get dad to come and see him.

I started to head back down the hall to go meet up with my dad who said he had to take something back to my mom's previous room, the one she was in before they took her to the ICU. I logged on to Facebook and posted a status stating that my mom is officially one of the most beautiful angels and how she would be forever mine. I began to imagine how I would still talk to her and write letters to her.

Still heading down the hall, I started to message people I knew lost their mothers in the past. I messaged my cousin, an old friend, and to each person I asked the same question. *What happens next and will I be sad forever?* Everyone gave a different answer, some people even responded to my post to share their experience with losing a parent. I really just needed to know what this process was going to look like so I could plan exactly how I was going to get through it.

Understanding Denial

Let's uncover denial. Earlier we defined denial as a defense mechanism that is employed to help minimize the pain of loss. These are a few traits to look for when identifying denial:

- Feeling emotionally numb.
- Forgetting about the loss.
- Shutting down or being unable to process emotions.
- Being confused and disoriented.
- Disbelief that the loss has occurred.

- Avoiding reminders of the loss.
- Staying busy all the time.
- Engaging in mindless behaviors and being easily distracted.
- Focusing on the needs of others instead of our own needs.
- Thinking or saying, *"I'm fine."* or *"Everything is fine."*

This list is not exhaustive and we must understand that denial can manifest itself in many different ways. However, it paints a picture of what a person in denial may be experiencing. While some of these may resonate with you I want you to also understand that denial is not a stage that we have to stay in, but recognizing it, is the first step to overcoming it.

Before we jump back into my story I'd like to give a few scriptures on what the Bible says about denial. While we may not see specific versus dedicated to denial, the Lord is very clear about the mind, and denial takes residence in the mind.

In Isaiah 26:3 the word of God says,

"You will keep in perfect peace all who trust in You, all whose thoughts are fixed on you."

I also love The Passion Translation *"Perfect, absolute peace surrounds those whose imaginations are consumed with You; they confidently trust in Him."* The issue with denial is that it essentially creates a shield that hides us from the truth, but it cannot last. In this scripture God offers to us everlasting, perfect peace that will continually surround us IF we fix our mind on Him.

When we are in denial we create our own way of escape, but God has already designed a way for us to retreat into Him.

Let's look at what Psalm 91: 1-2 (TPT) says,

"When you abide under the shadow of Shaddai, you are hidden in the strength of God Most High. He's the hope that holds me and the stronghold to shelter me, the only God for me, and my great confidence."

God was always intended to be the safe place for us to hide when we are afraid, when we don't understand, or when we don't want to face what we are experiencing. When we retreat to the recesses of our mind, we allow the thing that God wants us to hand over to Him to bury itself deep within our soul, only to manifest at usually inappropriate times. We will go into this more later, but it wasn't until about three years later that everything I shoved into a box and hid in the back of my mind began to manifest. Let me tell you, when it all finally came to the surface, it was not pretty.

As we get back to the story, let's look at how some of these traits of denial manifested in me. Feeling emotionally numb came over me instantly. I didn't have time to allow in or to feel the emotions that I knew would overtake me if I had let them. As much as I wanted to cry I shut it off and continued to head back down the hallway to see my dad walking past my mom's room with a cart. *"Dad"*, I yelled down the hall to get his attention so he'd know I was right behind him. I looked outside my mom's door and saw the get well soon balloon that I bought her just a day or two earlier. My dad also saw the balloon and he froze for a moment. I looked at him and said, *"It's going to be okay dad"*, in the strongest firmest voice I could muster up. My dad began to sob and I grabbed him to hug him and let him know that it was going to be okay.

As sad as this was, I couldn't allow myself to think any other thing except that it would be okay, and we just had to move forward. Fast forward to when we went home that night, there was an eerie silence that fell over the house. I honestly don't think anyone had any idea what to say. This was even the first time that all of us had been under one roof again in a long time. My dad had gone straight up to his room, I heard him make a few phone calls, but then something else happened. I heard the bath water run.

When my mom was alive she was very faithful to take a bath each night. It was something that she always asked us to do, run her some bath water. It was always something that I enjoyed, watching the bubbles fill the tub, then getting to press the jets. That night I heard the bath water run time after time after time again. I started to feel a little bit worried for my dad because I could only imagine the overwhelming sadness he felt as a thirty-five-year marriage came to an end. My brother must have been worried too because he decided to sleep on the floor outside of my parents' bedroom door. We all huddled downstairs together in the same room to sleep. I didn't sleep that night; in fact, I didn't sleep for days. Some of my siblings cried, some of them asked questions, some sought solace in friends.

I just remember laying there in wonder of how everyone else was going to get through this. For all intents and purposes, I had shut down and all I could do was what was required of me. Plan the funeral, get my family through. With the planning of the service, I stayed busy, I got to focus on the needs of everyone else, and I got to say *"I'm fine"* more times than I ever had before. I had gotten so good at declaring how fine I was it was always the same thing, "yes it hurts, but it will get better" I would say, never actually acknowledging the fact that my entire world had shifted and would never be the same again.

Denial can seem easier, but denial doesn't teach us how to grow through the change of loss. Processing our emotions is the only way that we adapt to what has just happened. For a while after my mom died I was seeing a therapist who tried to get me to process the pain but I told him it was much easier not to because I had "too much to do". It was three long years of denial and shoving the pain away. It's not to say that I didn't cry for three years. From time to time a tear or two would fall, but that was literally all I would allow myself. I'd give myself a moment to feel it and then I'd move on to whatever I was doing before. It kind of reminds me of when you shake up a bottle of soda and you slowly open it to release some of the carbonation so that it doesn't come spilling out all over the place.

You open it up just a bit, release some air, and then close it, and again and again until the bubbles have settled. I did this for a very long time. In the Bible we see many examples of loss. One of which is when King David loses his son that was born from his affair. Let's take a look at II Samuel 12:15-23:

"Then Nathan went home. And the Lord caused the baby boy who was born to David and Uriah's wife to become very sick. David prayed to God for the baby. David refused to eat or drink. He went into his house and stayed there and lay on the ground all night. The leaders of David's family came and tried to pull David up from the ground, but he refused to get up. He refused to eat with these leaders. On the seventh day the baby died. David's servants were afraid to tell him that the baby was dead. They said, "Look, we tried to talk to David while the baby was alive, but he refused to listen to us. If we tell David that the baby is dead, he might do something bad to himself." David saw his servants whispering and understood that the baby was dead. So, David asked his servants, "Is the baby dead?" The servants answered, "Yes, he is dead." Then David got up from the floor. He washed himself.

He changed his clothes and got dressed. Then he went into the Lord's house to worship. After that he went home and asked for something to eat. His servants gave him some food, and he ate. David's servants asked him, "Why are you doing this? When the baby was alive, you cried and refused to eat. But when the baby died you got up and ate food."

David said, "While the baby was still living, I cried and refused to eat because I thought, 'Who knows? Maybe the Lord will feel sorry for me and let the baby live.' But now the baby is dead, so why should I refuse to eat? Can I bring the baby back to life? No. Someday I will go to him, but he cannot come back to me." 2 Samuel 12:15-23 ERV

Overcoming Denial

The first step in overcoming denial that I briefly mentioned earlier is acknowledging that the loss has happened. Though in my case I knew that the loss occurred, I was doing everything in my power not to focus on it or the emotions that were trying to come. In this story we see that David was lamenting before experiencing the loss of his child because he was hoping that through his fasting and downcast posture that God would feel sorry for him and spare the life of the baby. However, we later see that this was not the case and unfortunately the child died. David's servants were worried about telling him that the baby died for fear of his reaction.

Something that we see here is that David was believing and hoping that God would do something, despite his wrongdoing. I personally related to this because I knew that the root of the denial I chose to fall into was that I was disappointed in God.

Here in this story however, there was a big difference in David's response versus mine. While David's servants did attempt to keep the truth from him, amongst their whispering David already discerned what was going on. David then asked if the child is dead, to which his servants tell him *"yes"*. Next we see David get up from the floor, wash himself, change his clothes, and ask for something to eat. The reason his servants were shocked was because he spent so much time lamenting that they assumed the death of the child would bring a greater depression.

What I love was David's response, though it probably took his servants by surprise. David spoke to them saying that even if he stayed on the floor and refused to eat the child would still be gone, and that eventually he would go to be with him but that the child would never come back to him. David recognized that while he likely still felt sad there was not much good in refusing to acknowledge what had happened.

Even more so David knew that looking toward the future would be more beneficial to him because he knew one day he would see the child again.

In 1 Thessalonians 4:13-14 the Bible says,

"Beloved brothers and sisters, we want you to be quite certain about the truth concerning those who have passed away, so that you won't be overwhelmed with grief like many others who have no hope. For if we believe that Jesus died and rose again, we also believe that God will bring with Jesus those who died while believing in him."

While this text is regarding the second coming of Jesus Christ, it gives us a glimpse into what we as believers can hope for when our loved ones die in Christ. It also helps us to understand where David's hope comes from. As believers we don't mourn the way the world does because if your loved one has died in the Lord we will see them again, and so we are able to look towards the future. Of course, it's not to say that it makes it hurt any less. However, if we hold on to hope we are less likely to fall into denial. So, the second step to overcoming denial is to look towards the future by placing your hope in Jesus Christ.

Here are a few practical steps to help you overcome denial:

1. ***Acknowledge that it has happened.***
    - You can journal about how you are handling what has happened and take that moment to talk to God.
    - You can also talk to those you trust, someone who is godly counsel, or even a professional counselor to help process the event.

2. ***Place your hope in Jesus.***
    - Meditate on the word of God. Begin to fill yourself with what God says about having hope.
    - Read a bible plan or a daily devotion about hope.

Here are some scriptures you can meditate on:

"Why, my soul, are you downcast? Why so disturbed within me? Put your hope in God, for I will yet praise him, my Savior and my God." Psalm 42:5 NIV

"Yes, my soul, find rest in God; my hope comes from him." Psalm 62:5 NIV

"And we know that in all things God works for the good of those who love him, who have been called according to his purpose." Romans 8:28 NIV

"But those who hope in the Lord will renew their strength. They will soar on wings like eagles; they will run and not grow weary; they will walk and not be faint." Isaiah 40:31 NIV

These are just a few and while you begin to meditate on the word of God I want you to remember that it's a big deal that you are choosing to acknowledge the loss. Opening that door for our Lord and Savior to walk into means that healing is on the way, joy is on the way, and peace is on the way. I am proud of you.

As we get further in this book, I want you to understand that God will be with you through every stage of this loss and all loss. Though I found myself deep in denial, looking back now I still wrote letters to God. I still wanted Him to stay close to me. Even in the midst of it all, I watched God carry my family through as they acknowledged what happened. Before we move into the next chapter I want to tell you a story about the day of my mom's funeral.

At the repass, when everyone comes together after the funeral to eat and basically fellowship, it was a very sad time as people attempted to comfort me and my family. There was a moment where we were all outside just talking and my brother who was still a senior in high school comes running outside of the house yelling. *"I got in. I got in."* he yelled at the top of his lungs as we all surrounded him. "What's going on?", my dad asked. My little brother began to read out loud his acceptance letter with a full scholarship to Howard University. Everyone, including me, began to praise him in roars of excitement. People began to say, *"He did it Rochelle"* or *"Your mom is looking down smiling".*

Even as I recall this story, tears fill my eyes because I remember very clearly looking towards heaven and quietly whispering *"Thank you God".* I knew that this was what my family needed and that this was the break in the waves that we had all been waiting for. I knew that this was...hope.

Let's Pray

Father, I thank You that even though the pain of loss is beyond what we can imagine or bare at times, that You're always right there to see us through. I ask you to come into this moment of grief and sorrow that is being hidden because the reality of letting it in is far too overwhelming and to give Your child rest. I thank you that Your arms are open and ready to bring comfort to the reader and that even the tears they cry are counted by You, letting us know that You're not distant and You have not forsaken or abandoned them in their sorrow, but You are right there. Help them to surrender any denial of this loss to You, as you grab hold of their hand and lead them into a journey of healing.

In Jesus name, Amen.

3

Anger

Something I've learned about anger the older I get is, that anger can be a tricky emotion and the root of a lot of what hinders us. Anger left unchecked always turns into unforgiveness and bitterness, and we almost always end up creating walls that nobody can get over…including God. Anger also has an uncanny ability to masks itself under the cover of many other emotions like fear or sadness. The real lie operating behind unchecked anger is that it's protecting us.

After my mom died, I carried a lot of anger in my heart and believe it or not it took me years to realize that anger was the root that led me down a dark path. The one thing I did not want to be after my mom died was angry. I wanted to be at peace with it and accept what God was doing. So, when I would think about how my mom died at 59 and never got to see the birth of any grandchildren or any of her children be married, I would stave off the anger, grit down on my teeth, and push it back into the box of all my other unchecked emotions.

Social media tends to get a glimpse into what probably should be private intimate moments, but it's also a space that people use to express themselves. So, as the days went on after my mom's passing I was posting a lot of different things. We had to go through all of the family albums in order to find pictures of my mom to put together for her obituary. My mom hated taking pictures so this was a task all in itself. When we found pictures some of them made us laugh, some of them surprised us, and some of them made my heart hurt, though I never told anyone that. I would screenshot the picture and post it on social media along with a message about how beautiful and amazing my mommy was. I'd post a status about how my family was doing, or how it was hard to sleep.

One day, this guy who I met online at some point in my college years, decided to go out of his way and comment something on one of those posts. What he essentially said was that I needed to get over it and that I didn't need to continue to post about it. This made me angry to my core. I was appalled and couldn't believe that me posting positive memories about my mother had offended him that much. I promptly deleted him without responding. Then I made a post about how no one who hasn't lost their parents, especially their mom, could possibly understand what I am going through.

I went on to say that you hold yourself together with tape and glue and you refer to her as if she were still alive, because you can barely stomach the idea of the world existing without her. I did receive a lot of responses about how I shouldn't allow people's ignorance to bother me, but this was the first time that I really acknowledged that I was angry and I couldn't shove it aside. I read that status that I posted over and over again thinking to myself, *he doesn't even know that I still refer to her as if she's still here. He doesn't know what it takes to endure this loss.* As I repeatedly read that post,

I felt the tears attempt to fill my eyes as the anger raged on. Several deep breaths later, I let it go and decided that I would post whatever I needed to in order to remember my mom the way I needed to.

After my mom's funeral I felt the anger rage on again as people would send me texts asking to have a garment of her clothing or go through her pictures. I was still in this space trying to preserve my mom's memories and I couldn't believe that nobody could see the error of their timing. Truthfully it may seem small, but it actually took time to forgive those people. Glory be to God that He has taught me how to forgive and love even after pain. The denial wasn't driving the pain in my heart but the anger was, as people called to constantly remind me that she was no longer alive.

To this day, I never gave anything away. By the time the anger passed, there was a season where 70% of my family did not even speak anymore.

Being angry at my family was easy. The entire time I felt as if nobody really could possibly understand what it felt like to watch my dad grieve or feel the confusion that swept the room each day as we tried to peace our lives back together.

The hard part was being angry with God. Something to note about my relationship with God, it's always been the greatest experience of love for me. If you know me, I always refer to Him as the lover of my soul. During the grief I wanted to press deeper into this love. I didn't want to acknowledge that I had been hurt by the One I loved the most. Realizing I was angry with my family wasn't at all subtle, it was fast and hard and full of contempt. Realizing I was angry with God was a process that slowly rolled out over time, until one day He spoke to me and said, *"you're mad at me."*

I think it took me so long to acknowledge my disappointment in God because you always hear people say, never question God, or you can't have feelings towards God when someone dies. Let me be very clear, me being mad with God did not take away the tremendous love I have for Him. It just made it hurt a little.

I think it took me so long to acknowledge my disappointment in God because you always hear people say, never question God, or you can't have negative feelings towards God when someone dies. Let me be very clear, me being mad with God did not take away the tremendous love I have for Him. It just made it hurt a little. It took about five years for me to see the anger manifest. Here's a brief walk down those five years of what that anger looked like and maybe you can identify yourself as well.

The first time the anger manifested was the first time I tried to go back to work. It was about 2 weeks after my mom passed. Working in behavioral therapy, which is work with autistic kids. I worked in the school setting and also in the home. I pulled up to the school that morning ready to get my head off of everything that had happened. Suddenly, I heard this swarm of small children yelling around me, *"mom", "I love you mommy", "bye mom".* I felt my heart drop as the first angry thought went across my mind; *I don't have a mom anymore.* I wanted to be sad; this was a sad thought but all I felt was this fire burning inside me. I wanted to run and leave that place as quickly as possible because here I was angry, jealous of small children that they got to say things that I would never get to say again.

Needless to say, I did not make it through that day.

In fact, I made it only 30 minutes before I let the teacher know I couldn't do it and bolted. I got into my car with the same notion of habit that I got into it with each time. I wanted to call my mom. It had become a part of my routine. I get into my car and I call my mom. If I was on lunch break I would call her, on my way home I would call her, and this morning the reflex came rising up all the same. I got so angry because I felt dumb remembering that she was no longer available. I pounded my fist on the steering wheel as a tear fell from my eye. I wiped it away quickly and focused on the road home.

Understanding Anger

There's being angry and we will talk about the signs of that. You can also be angry with God and I am going to share what that looks like. The APA Dictionary of Psychology defines anger as an emotion characterized by tension and hostility arising from frustration, real or imagined injury by another, or perceived injustice. The portion of this definition that I would like to focus on is the "perceived injustice".

Sometimes when we experience loss it can automatically feel as though we were wronged, placing blame is almost certainly the easiest thing to do.

Being angry with God seems to be the easier form of anger after you experience a great loss. Our loved one gets killed by a drunk driver; we blame God. Thousands are killed and lives upended by a natural disaster, we blame God. A campus shooter takes the lives of children that we know and love, we blame God. The point is not to minimize the severity of the devastation left behind from such events, but to highlight the fact that God is usually the first person who takes the blame. In these situations, sometimes we do get a picture of a clear person to blame like the drunk driver, the mass shooter, or mother nature. What happens when our loved ones pass peacefully in the night at 29 years old or lose the fight to juvenile diabetes like my mom? Who gets the bill of blame then?

It's human nature for us to want to assign blame because we need a place to plant our flag of anger. There were so many people that I could have directed my anger towards, but I didn't need anything from them, honestly I didn't care. But God was my friend.

Here are some telltale signs that you may be experiencing anger with God:

- **The language you use towards Him directs blame.**

About three years after my mom passed I had a nervous breakdown.

I woke up one morning with this tremendous pressure in my head and with the help of the enemy's deceiving hand, I decided I was dying. For the next three weeks I would visit hospital after hospital with the same story, I am dying. I would enter the emergency room having a full-blown panic attack with a blood pressure of 155 over 90, which is not normal for a 27-year-old female. *"See, I'm having a heart attack. Something is wrong with me"*, I would cry to the triage nurse. *"Do you have a history of heart problems?"*, the nurse asked, holding my hand asking me to take a deep breath. *"No, I don't know...my mom...my mom..."* I said, the tears falling, as I felt the breath leaving my body each time I explained. *"Something was wrong with my mom's heart, she died. God let my mom die."*, I cried.

This trend went on for the course of three weeks, hospital after hospital, *"God let my mom die."*, I would say. For the next few years, I was absolutely convinced that He was going to let me die too. I didn't want to pray to Him. Was He even listening? As I continued to experience this panic over the next few weeks, I would confide in leaders at my church, asking them for prayer and wisdom. I would try to get into the presence of God, but I just didn't trust Him.

So instead of the posture of a daughter, I began to take the posture of a beggar. I would do anything, but we will discuss bargaining later. Another clear sign that followed the anger I felt toward God was the lack of trust.

- **You stop trusting God or you lose hope in what He can do for you.**

This may not look the same for everyone, but as God started to reveal to me my anger, this was a sign that followed. A lot of times when we are angry with someone it shifts our ability to trust them. We say things like *"I just don't trust them with my heart"* or *"they did me wrong, so they don't have my best interest at heart"*. Proverbs 13:12 says, *"Hope deferred makes the heart sick, but when the desire comes it is a tree of life."*

When our hope and trust in God is misplaced it can seem as though all our dreams and all of our desires go somewhere to die. I was certain He planned on me dying as well. So, there was no reason to believe. Amidst all of this chaos of going back and forth to the hospital and crisis centers, I eventually was encouraged to check myself into a crisis residential treatment center for 30 days. Part of my stay was that I had to attend several lessons throughout the day, whether that be a class on anger, a rec and leisure class, yoga or exercise. I had to stay plugged in.

One of the weird things that happened to me was I started to become fearful of doing anything related to the future. In one of the rec and leisure classes we could paint our nails, or do a face mask, or something relaxing while we focus on mindfulness. I quite literally could not do this, because anytime I pictured painting my nails I would picture myself in a casket with those same nails. My thought was *these are probably going to be the nails God lets me die in.* Truly, my heart was sick. I was exhausted and full of fear. This went on for a very long time and it wasn't until I forgave God, that it broke and I put on some make up and bought a pair of lashes. I still texted my cousin and said, *"if I die can you make sure I have lashes on?"* Needless to say, the healing took a while.

You may have noticed that I mentioned something you don't usually hear. I had to forgive God. First, let me express that God did nothing wrong.

The word of God says,

"*God is not a man, that He should lie, Nor a son of man, that He should repent. Has He said, and will He not do? or has He spoken and will He not make it good?* Numbers 23:19 NKJV

I didn't have to forgive God because He did something wrong. I had to forgive God because anger had sown a root of bitterness in my soul and it was directed at God. It was not as blatantly obvious at first, but there was a moment that God revealed to me that He was on the list of people that I needed to forgive.

Fast forward to 2022, I had joined a new church. Part of something that we do at this church is take classes that are designed to help with our spiritual development. In the class that is focused on freedom in Christ, there is a week where we talk about forgiveness. While I was in that class, we were asked to work through forgiving all the people that God highlighted for us. As I was writing down all of the names, I stood up as instructed to go over my list and I heard the quietest voice speak to me. "*You need to forgive me*", He said.

Then He proceeded to tell me how much He loved me. I started to feel this overwhelming sadness welling up in me. Had I really been so disconnected from God because I blamed Him for taking my mom away? Under my breath I let the words out, *"God, I forgive You for taking my mom when you did, and I'm sorry that I have been angry with you for so long"*. I fell to my knees and sobbed. I started to get a vision of how my life with God was about to change.

We serve a loving Father, one full of mercy, compassion, and unending grace. Me not forgiving God was a stronghold put in place by the devil that fortified the lie that He wasn't good. Even though we experience the pain of loss and things don't always seem fair, we must recognize the sovereignty of God. That word sovereign basically means that God is control of all things and rules over all things. God has power and authority over all things, in fact there is nothing that happens that doesn't first pass through the hands of God. Guess what? Even in all of that it doesn't change His goodness, it doesn't change that He is the embodiment of unconditional love. It's us that changes, and us that make mistakes. It's us who get angry with a perfect loving God. It took God addressing the anger in me for me to put who He is back into perspective so I can experience the fullness of a relationship with Him. I want to encourage you to put God back into the proper perspective by realizing that He isn't the blame for the loss, or the pain you feel from the loss.

I want you to let this scripture soak into your heart:

"The Lord is close to all whose hearts are crushed by pain, and he is always ready to restore the repentant one. Even when bad things happen to the good and godly ones, the Lord will save them and not let them be defeated by what they face." Psalms 34:18-19 TPT

In your brokenness and in your anger, God is right there. Being angry with Him is a trap set to keep you bound and blocked off from the real healing God wants to bring you. Release God from the idea of what loss has made you believe.

Maybe you aren't experiencing anger at God.

Let's discuss some characteristics that indicate that you may be experiencing anger:

- Feeling impatient
- Being pessimistic or cynical
- Engaging in self-harm
- Being short tempered and emotionally unstable
- Being verbally or physically aggressive
- Having thoughts such as *"this isn't fair", "no one understands", "they deserve to pay", or "I want revenge"*

Again, this list is not exhaustive, but these are some fair indicators that you may be experiencing anger.

Overcoming Anger

Anger is a normal part of grieving; the goal is to make sure you don't stay there. In the Bible the example is Job. If you have not read the book of Job yet, I encourage you to do so because he of all people understands what it means to experience loss.

For context, Job was a faithful and righteous man of God who went through a serious trial. Job experienced the loss of his children, security and comfort, and his health. While Job was called righteous by God Himself, Job still reacted in grief through anger.

"After this, Job opened his mouth and cursed the day of his birth. He said: "May the day of my birth perish, and the night that said, 'A boy is conceived!' That day—may it turn to darkness; may God above not care about it; may no light shine on it. May gloom and utter darkness claim it once more; may a cloud settle over it; may blackness overwhelm it. That night—may thick darkness seize it; may it not be included among the days of the year nor be entered in any of the months. May that night be barren; may no shout of joy be heard in it." Job 3:1-7 NIV

"Why did I not perish at birth, and die as I came from the womb?" Job 3:11 NIV

Job cursing the day that he was born is indicative of what I stated about self-harm and destructive thoughts such as *"Why is this happening to me?"* Job no longer saw the point in his living because if he knew he was going to encounter the day that he experienced such a tremendous loss, he would rather not have been born at all.

Have you felt like that in this season of grief? I did. I mostly couldn't understand how God could give me someone that I would love so much and then take her away.

Job was angry. Job did not want to exist anymore. I also would like to point out something interesting. You don't have to be the only person who is angry. There are people around you who may be filled with anger and try to project that anger onto you. Before we go over to chapter 7 let's look at an example of this.

Job's wife in chapter two literally told him to curse God and die, in fact she asked him *"Why are you still trying to hold on to your integrity?"*

"Then his wife said to him, "Do you still hold fast to your integrity? Curse God and die!" Job 2:9 NKJV

Job's wife is the perfect example of what not to do! This is why it's important that you work through overcoming your anger, especially if it's with God.

To the point also in this time of grieving, surround yourself with people who are going to encourage you and build you up, not tell you to just curse God and die. You need to surround yourself with people that can speak life and that see light at the end of the tunnel.

"Therefore, I will not keep silent; I will speak out in the anguish of my spirit, I will complain in the bitterness of my soul." Job 7:11 NIV

Job was filled with anger at his loss so much so that he refused to stop complaining and he refused to keep quiet about the bitterness that filled his soul. Job wasn't wrong in what he was feeling, he was allowed to be angry, he was even allowed to express it. Something I want to point out in the book of Job is that he had friends who corrected him and encouraged him in the Lord as we keep reading. Job went to God in his anger and in his feelings and spoke deeply to him about what he had been feeling. Job asked God if there was something he did

"Then call, and I will answer; Or let me speak, then You respond to me. How many are my iniquities and sins? Make me know my transgression and my sin." Job 13:22-23 NKJV

In all of this, Job also resolved in his heart that he would still put his faith and his trust in God.

"Though He slay me, yet will I trust in Him...." Job 13:15 KJV

Job had already resolved in his heart that even if God killed him, he was still going to place his hope in Him. This was the whole point of the scripture in that Satan thought that if Job were to face many dreadful trials that he would renounce God.

I know that what you're feeling is real, that the anger and disappointment sometimes wants to consume you, but I want to encourage you that the first practical step in overcoming this anger is to put your trust in God no matter what. Decide in your heart that even if everything were to be ripped from you today that you would still trust Him. This my friend is how we overcome all.

Here are some practical ways to help you and others overcome anger:

1. ***Allow yourself to feel the loss.***
   - The goal is not to just push back all the anger inside of you and hope it goes away but to process the way you're feeling in a healthy manner.
   - Our feelings are constantly changing, you won't always be angry. What we feel in a moment of grief isn't truth compared to God's word so it will not last. Don't be afraid to feel the anger. Take it to God, one prayer at a time.

2. ***Surround yourself with friends and family who will support you and what you're feeling and will pray with you through it and let you cry it out, scream it out, and feel your way through this loss.***
   - Don't surround yourself with people like Jobs` wife who would encourage you to curse God, or to drink it away or smoke it away or any other activity that's just going to give you temporary numbness.

3. ***Recognize the underlying feelings.***
   - Do you remember earlier when I mentioned sometimes anger likes to hide behind other feelings? Well, the same is true for other emotions like sadness, or depression. These emotions can be hidden away by a wall of anger.
   - It's important that you identify the underlying feelings so that you can begin to peel back the layers and start your healing.

4. ***Find healthy ways to express your emotions.***
   - It can be easy for the world to provide us with "coping skills" that aren't healthy or effective, that are simply band aids over bullet holes. Turning to substances, sex, and dangerous or risky activities will only bandage an issue that needs to be dealt with by a physician. The greatest physician of all is Jesus Christ.
   - Prayer and journaling are going to be one of the main sources of expressing your emotion because it's going to allow for a release that you will not get by pushing the feelings aside or sedating them.
   - Art, healthy physical activities such as swimming, riding a bike, going to the gym are all ways to experience a healthy release of emotions.

5. ***Work on changing your cycle of thinking.***
   - The Bible talks about taking every thought captive in 2 Corinthians 10:5 which can be easier said than done, I know. I want to encourage you to start to intercept the thoughts that lead you into feelings of deep anger and sadness with what the word of God says. By the end of this book, you will have an arsenal of scriptures you can use.
   - Let's create an example. You might have the thought *"God doesn't care about me because if He did He would not have let this happen"*. Intercept that thought with the truth.
   - God's word says, He has loved me with an everlasting love and with His love and kindness He draws me to Him. This scripture reference is Jeremiah 31:3.
   - Refuse to believe the lie that someone has to be blamed. Begin to shift the perspective of your thinking when encountering people and situations in this process of grief that the enemy may use to trigger that anger.
   - Allow yourself to see everything through a lens of compassion, towards yourself, towards others caught up in the grief, and towards God.

Here are the scriptures I want you to meditate on:

"We demolish arguments and every pretension that sets itself up against the knowledge of God, and we take captive every thought to make it obedient to Christ." 2 Corinthians 10:5 NIV

"The Lord appeared to us in the past, saying: "I have loved you with an everlasting love; I have drawn you with unfailing kindness." Jeremiah 31:3 NIV

"I pray that the light of God will illuminate the eyes of your imagination, flooding you with light, until you experience the full revelation of the hope of his calling —that is, the wealth of God's glorious inheritances that he finds in us, his holy ones! I pray that you will continually experience the immeasurable greatness of God's power made available to you through faith. Then your lives will be an advertisement of this immense power as it works through you! This is the mighty power." Ephesians 1:18-19 TPT

"I consider that our present sufferings are not worth comparing with the glory that will be revealed in us." Romans 8:18 NIV

Let's Pray:

Father, right now I just lift this reader up to You! I thank You that they will not be consumed by anger but by your loving kindness that You would draw them unto You. Let them know Your comfort and love that comes from pulling in close to You. I thank You that no matter what they are facing in this current life, that it doesn't even compare to what is later to be revealed to us. Help them to shift their perspective and to destroy every cycle of thinking that would keep them bound in anger. Set them free from every spirit and stronghold of anger rooted by this loss. I thank You that You never said that they would never experience anger, but that the anger doesn't have the authority to consume them. We release that anger to You right now and replace every feeling with Your truth.

In Jesus name, Amen.

4

Bargaining

In the very beginning of my journey as a Christian, I didn't fully understand what it meant to be saved. I knew that it meant that I wasn't going to hell, but I didn't experience what it was like to be in a relationship with God. A relationship with Him reveals our true identity of not having to earn our way into heaven. Believing that you need to earn your way into heaven is very much like bargaining.

After my mother passed away, I started trying to work my way into heaven. Before my mom passed, I had already tried to work on developing a relationship with Jesus and naturally with that some of my behaviors changed. I was no longer drinking, I stopped smoking, and the way I spoke started to change. As I mentioned earlier, I started trying to press myself deeper into that "relationship" that I had with God by showing up to church every Sunday, Bible study every Wednesday, spending time with my mentor, trying to live in this posture of joy, because Christian's have joy right? When I had my nervous breakdown, a shift began to happen because I started to feel like God had not been there.

I started to look back over the course of the prior months and about all the things I had done. I was showing up to church, I was praying every night, I wasn't smoking, I was trying my best not to drink, and I certainly wasn't having sex. *God where are you*? I thought to myself.

Right before my nervous breakdown, I lived in an apartment by myself and as I previously mentioned, I was already living there fueled with the fear that I was going to die by some massive tumor in my brain that nobody could find. But I was also consumed by the fear that someone was going to come into my apartment and hurt me or I would die and nobody would know. One night, I couldn't take it anymore. Nobody was answering their phone and I didn't want to run to the crisis center or the hospital. I started thinking maybe I'm not giving God the opportunity to help me. Side bar, I didn't know anything about being free in Christ or what that really meant, so of course I just thought something was really wrong with me.

Looking back, I needed freedom and it was finally sitting right there in that room on my shoulders and my soul was desperate. So, I got on my knees and I started crying, *"Jesus please, please help me, I can't do this anymore, what's wrong with me?"* I cried out.

My head fell into my lap and I began sobbing loudly and this thought came, maybe I need to get on my face. I knew when people were really serious about hearing from God or wanted to humble themselves before Him, they would lay prostrate before the Lord, which meant laying your face. So, I did that and I laid there crying into the carpet waiting for God to say something or to lift the fear off of me, so that I could go back to living life trying to do the right thing. I sat up from that spot and the pressure and dizziness and fear was still there. After that night, these thoughts started working in my head, *something is wrong with me, I've done something wrong, God is mad at me.* It was those thoughts that sent me into this next stage, bargaining.

I started to nurse the idea that I was being punished and that my mom died because I was being punished. I didn't want anyone else to die because of me, my dad, my brothers and sisters. I knew that I had to take my Christianity into overtime and so I decided that I was just going to focus on God.

Fear started to grow that at any moment if I did anything wrong, if I even sneezed too hard, someone else was going to die and it was all on me.

Understanding Bargaining

The APA Dictionary of psychology defines bargaining as an attempt to negotiate a deal with God or fate that would delay one's own death, or that of an important other person, or that would mitigate or end other great loss or trauma. This definition really stands out to me because it is an exact representation of everything I was experiencing in this stage. The part that stands out to me the most is that one would attempt to negotiate a deal with God that would mitigate or end great loss or trauma. After everything that I had already gone through, I could not fathom the idea of anymore trauma. I never wanted to feel this type of pain, confusion, or loss ever again. I wanted to be set free from this kind of pain.

Of course, I knew that this didn't mean that no one would ever die, because death is a natural part of life. I would negotiate with God like this, *"Lord let me please have children before you take my dad"* or *"God please don't let anything happen to my siblings because I promise to always show up"*. I made promises to God that I would show up and be there for my family and friends and the people who loved me, that I would stretch myself out over time as much as was needed, but please just don't take anyone else.

There were times, and even as I gained more maturity in Christ, my phone would ring and I would jump with fear and anxiety and quickly answer the phone because I was afraid that someone was going to tell me that someone else died. Before I would even answer my phone I would begin to bargain with God, *"Lord please let everything be okay, please let everything be okay"*.

As I mentioned earlier, all of this landed me in a crisis residential treatment center and even while I was in there, I remember just apologizing to God over and over and over again. This was not a repentant apology, this was a plea filled with guilt, make this stop, I'm sorry. \It wasn't even that I wasn't sorry for my sin or for the wrong that I had done up until this point, because I was.

I truly believed that God was mad at me for so much more than that. The only goal that I had at that point was to mitigate that punishment. My goal was to lessen my sentence. I even remember thinking that my mom died because I was too close to her. I wondered if it was because I depended on her more than I depended on God. I kept having this running conversation with God about when I got out of here. *"In the next 30 days, when I get out of here, I'm never going to drink again"*, I would say. *"When I get out of here, "I promise I won't have sex again until I'm married"* I'd tell Him.

I started to make promises to God. *"Every morning God I'm going to wake up and pray, I'm going to give you the first of my day, it's going to be just like it used to be."* I'd say, trying to reassure even myself.

Sometime after losing my mom, my dad actually ended up getting sick, he was diagnosed with cancer. All I could think was *"Oh my God, here we go again."* This was something that happened before I even had the nervous breakdown. But I was sitting in the waiting room waiting for him and I started negotiating with God. *"Lord please don't take my dad, you just took my mom, I'll do anything"*, I said. I told God that I would be a better person, I would be nicer, I would do whatever He wanted me to do.

The reason we negotiate with God after experiencing such trauma is because we start to feel as though we have nothing left. It's almost like all we have left is our leverage. It's the only thing remaining that we can control. Before I go any farther I want to let you know that you don't have to leverage God. Us losing our control can sometimes feel like the worst thing, because it brings worry, anxiety, and it doesn't feel good. It's important in this stage to look at God and all of His sovereignty and realize that He is still in control and it's okay to let Him be. We can talk more about how to overcome this stage, but how do you know you're bargaining?

Here are some characteristics of bargaining:

- Feeling guilty about your thoughts or actions
- Feeling scared, insecure, or anxious
- Punishing yourself
- Holding yourself responsible for what happened
- Trying to predict the future and expecting the worst

What's significant about all of these characteristics is that they all point back to you having some monumental part in this loss and the remedy for future losses. Let me take some of that burden off of you and let you know that there was nothing you did wrong and there's nothing you can do to change the future or anyone's life except your own. By this I mean, put down the burden of thinking that there is something wrong with you, or that the loss you're experiencing is somehow a catalyst of something awful you've done.

It's also not true that any action you could have taken would have prevented this loss. This is where we have to address control again. God is in control. So, release yourself from the mindset that says, *"if only I was there", "if only I showed up sooner",* or *"if I tried harder"*. When you are overcome with this kind of guilt, you're saying that you have to make up for all the wrong you've done.

Before I share the signs that you may be trying to bargain with God, here's a familiar verse in the Bible where we see an example of bargaining.

"Then Jesus went with his disciples to a place called Gethsemane, and he said to them, "Sit here while I go over there and pray." He took Peter and the two sons of Zebedee along with him, and he began to be sorrowful and troubled. Then he said to them, "My soul is overwhelmed with sorrow to the point of death. Stay here and keep watch with me." Going a little farther, he fell with his face to the ground and prayed, "My Father, if it is possible, may this cup be taken from me. Yet not as I will, but as you will." Matthew 26:36-39 NIV

In the verse above, Jesus is preparing Himself to go to the cross and before that He goes the Garden of Gethsemane to pray. Jesus was about to experience the greatest loss of all, His life.

Jesus pointed out that His soul was overwhelmed with sorrow and the thought of going through the pain that He was set to experience on the cross was probably agonizing to Him. So, Jesus says to His father, if it is possible, let this cup pass from me. Jesus was asking God to spare Him from this suffering.

In our previous definition, bargaining is a deal made in an attempt to delay one's own death.

While of course Jesus was not outright making a deal with God, He's expressing to Him a plea asking God if He would pass this responsibility away from Him. When we are bargaining that's exactly what we are doing. We are taking the wheel and saying, *Lord please pass by me, pass by my family, and pass by my friends.*

The reason I chose this scripture is for the very next line, that Jesus says, "*Yet not as I will, but as you will.*" Jesus knew that He was going to experience this pain and that loss was going to come and even though He wanted God to take it away, He made a choice to say, *Lord let your will be done.* Jesus let go of the wheel and placed the control back into the hands of the person who is sovereign over everything.

How do you know you're bargaining with God?

- You agree to do things that you think would please Him enough to pass over you.
- You take on the role of fault in what's going to transpire around you..
- You take the posture of a beggar.

We are sinners saved by grace, so what we have to offer to God will unfortunately never be enough. When you're bargaining with God, you fall into that work-based mentality, which is sure to wear you out, make you feel insecure, and create mistrust in God. Imagine you're a child and your parents love you so much, naturally because you're their child right? Let's assume that there's absolutely nothing that you can do to make them love you anymore than they do.

Something happens and you start trying to do everything in YOUR power to please them. You start cleaning the kitchen three times a day, you do the laundry twice a week, you never get in trouble, you join every sport and try to win every trophy possible, you even get straight A's. For some reason it seems like they don't notice, and you're exhausted. You start to feel insecure because now you're taking on the identity that you're not enough, you don't really even trust or believe that they love you, because they just aren't noticing anything you're doing.

This is the same thing that happens when we start bargaining with God and trying to "work" for Him! God already loves you, not because of what you can do for Him. God's plans and His will are already done for your life, not because of what you did or did not do.

God does not make decisions about your life based on how well you please Him. Do you want to know what moves God? Faith moves God. In the Garden of Gethsemane Jesus placed His faith back in the rightful place, in God. Having faith won't even negate the fact that loss is hard, learning to live without someone you love is hard, but faith makes it possible. Faith in God will bring forth a peace in your heart that trying to figure it out on your own cannot.

The next indicator of bargaining with God is taking on the role or fault in future events. The problem with carrying guilt after losing a loved one is that guilt, like anger, like sadness, and any other deep-seated emotion, messes with your perspective. Do you remember how earlier I promised God that I would show up for my family if he just took care of them? That guilt that fueled my bargaining had me carrying my family around in a glass bubble, fearful that even the slightest thing I did would be the reason something happened to one of them.

Overcoming Bargaining

Before I began writing this book, there was an incident that happened. I essentially got scammed into thinking someone kidnapped my sister; believe me it was awful. I was on the phone for hours negotiating with this alleged kidnapper, begging, and pleading with friends for money to pay her ransom. Not once, until I allowed the Holy Spirit to speak to me, did I even consider it was a scam. Do you know why? Because I was still carrying my family around in this space of delicacy. Mind you, this is going on almost seven years after losing my mother, and while I was no longer bargaining with God because now we have a relationship, God had to show me that I still needed to surrender my family to Him.

The worst part of this ordeal was the fear that consumed me, to the point where I ended up needing deliverance right after. The one thing that stood out right where that fear was planting its flag was that if I hung up the phone, if I said the wrong thing, if I asked for help and the alleged kidnapper found out, I'd cost my sister her life. All over again in a matter of hours the enemy was trying to take me back to a place that I knew God had freed me from.

So, when I learned that my sister was not actually in the back of a van being driven to Mexico to be trafficked, as the man told me, I'm sitting there after having leaders help me through deliverance and I realize that the reason the enemy wants us to carry guilt and to think that somehow we have influence to be the ruin of everyone's life, or the cause of death for people and even things around us like our careers or relationship, is because he's after one thing, our identity.

Now I know you might be saying, wait, Nichelle, what does my identity have to do with the guilt I feel or the fact that if I say one wrong thing I'm going to lose someone else? When we carry guilt we forget who we are. When we look down at our hands and see death and destruction, we forget that we are children of the Creator of EVERYTHING. It's very hard to have faith and to trust God when you feel like nothing more than a failure and a cause for destruction. Can I impart something to you today as you take one giant step out of this distortion of your identity that says you have to beg your Father, or that your hands are anything but life giving?

When you gave your life to Jesus Christ, He reached down and took you out of the pit and brought you into the palace.

It's important for you to know who you are so that you never walk as a beggar again. You have access to the King of Kings and the Lord of Lords; you are a son or daughter of the Most High.

"And you did not receive the "spirit of religious duty," leading you back into the fear of never being good enough. But you have received the "Spirit of full acceptance," enfolding you into the family of God. And you will never feel orphaned, for as he rises up within us, our spirits join him in saying the words of tender affection, "Beloved Father!" Romans 8:15 TPT

You're a child of the most Beloved Father and so it's okay to give Him the guilt that you've been feeling. This was not your fault and God doesn't want you trying to barter with Him to seal the fates of yourself and those you love. You don't have to live afraid of what could be. Maybe you're reading this and you don't know Jesus, maybe you've never actually invited Him into your life to be your Beloved Father.

Maybe you're reading this and you walked away from God and you don't see Him as your Father, but you want to restore that relationship. Don't worry, at the end of this chapter we are going to pray together and restore you to your rightful place in the Kingdom of God.

First, let's discuss practical way to overcome the bargaining stage:

1. ***Shift your perspective to a Kingdom perspective***
   - This might look like meditating on scriptures about who you are in Christ, and scriptures that reveal the character of God. I'm going to share some scriptures that meet that criteria but I also encourage you to google search scriptures that have to do with those two things and create a list that you can refer to when you start to feel like a burden in the kingdom rather than a blessing.
   - When you're able to finally see who you are in Christ, you won't feel so burdened with the thought of bargaining with God because you'll realize that as a child of the King you have everything you need. Peace? He has that! Joy? He has that too! Freedom? He has it! And it's all open to you.

2. ***Give yourself time***
   - Do you remember earlier when I mentioned that it's been seven years and sometimes I still have to remember not to carry my family like fragile China dolls? Grief is not an exact science, sometimes it takes time.

- It's okay to allow yourself one day at a time to remember that God has your best interest at heart and that You can trust Him with your prayers and don't have to leverage Him to have hope.
- Give yourself grace and don't be so hard on yourself.

3. ***It's okay not to hold on so tightly.***
    - Just as much as God loves you, He also loves your family and friends. It's okay to let God do the hard work of making sure that they stay safe.
    - Sometimes our families and friends can seem so delicate after a situation of loss and we want to hold to them ever so tightly. However, think about what happens when you hold on to a butterfly too tightly, we end up doing more harm than good.
    - It's okay to let our family's grow and bloom in front of our eyes and be proud of what we see. No more imagining the worse!

Now, here are the scriptures that will help restore your identity and remind you who Christ is:

"And before the world was made, God decided to make us his own children through Jesus Christ. This was what God wanted, and it pleased him to do it." Ephesians 1:5 ERV

"Therefore, as God's chosen people, holy and dearly loved, clothe yourselves with compassion, kindness, humility, gentleness and patience." Colossians 3:12 NIV

"But you are his chosen people, the King's priests. You are a holy nation, people who belong to God. He chose you to talk about the wonderful things he has done. He brought you out of the darkness of sin into his wonderful light." 1 Peter 2:9 ERV

"With Jesus as our high priest, we can feel free to come before God's throne where there is grace. There we receive mercy and kindness to help us when we need it." Hebrews 4:16 ERV

"The Lord passed in front of Moses, calling out, "Yahweh! The Lord! The God of compassion and mercy! I am slow to anger and filled with unfailing love and faithfulness." Exodus 34:6 NLT

"God's way is perfect. The Lord's promise always proves to be true. He protects those who trust in him." Psalms 18:30 ERV

Let's pray

If you haven't yet received Jesus as your Lord and savior or you want to invite Him back into your heart lets pray this together.

Lord, I am sorry for shifting my heart away from You. I'm sorry that I've lived a life without You at the center of it. I believe everything that You did for me. I believe that You lived and died on the cross. I believe that You rose on the third day with all power in Your hands. I ask You to come into my heart and be Lord and Savior over my life. I surrender my life to You, Jesus. I know that as Your child I don't have to beg You for anything. I know that You desire to take care of me and my family and friends. So, God I put down the need to work for You or to bargain with You and I trust you with my life. I trust you with the lives of my family and friends. Show me who I am in Your kingdom. Take away every false image that would make me take the posture of a beggar and raise me up as a son or daughter. Thank you Lord.

In Jesus name, Amen.

5

Depression

After all the denial, anger, and bargaining, I think the hardest thing to encounter when it comes to grief is depression. The thing about depression is it has an awful way of being all consuming. I closed all the blinds and all the shades, put my head under the covers, play the saddest song I can think of on repeat, and refuse to leave my bed for any reason other than to use the bathroom.

I remember the depression stage quite well. Depression did not hit me until a few years after my mother passed. I was on this high of staying busy and doing work for God and refusing to cry for longer than 5 minutes at a time. When depression finally did hit me, it was in fact all-consuming and I saw my addiction come to fruition. It's not that I wasn't sad and didn't have moments, but I don't believe I was truly depressed yet. I had experienced depression for many years before my mom passed, so I was very familiar with the feeling. In college I felt like I was in a dark pit 90% of the time and all I wanted to do was drink, party, and forget that the crippling darkness that I felt was even real.

I think that's why losing my mom I was so fearful to allow the fullness of that grief to hit me because I thought well what could be worse than the darkness that I had previously felt, death? I mean I was truly convinced that I would die the moment I allowed that sorrow and sadness that waited for me to come in.

The depression stage is usually identified by sadness, loss, or regret following a death or major loss or impending death or major loss. This is essentially what the APA dictionary of psychology says about the depression stage.

However, something I also know from experience to be true about depression, is that sometimes when you're in it that it can feel like more than just run of the mill sadness. Part of a clinical diagnosis of depression and any of the mental health diagnoses in the DSM, is that it interferes with your daily life.

The definition of depression in the APA dictionary vs the depression stage is identified by extreme feelings of sadness, pessimism, and despondency that interferes with daily life. Psychical, cognitive, and social changes also occur such as altered eating or sleeping habits, lack of energy or motivation, difficulty concentrating or making decisions, and withdrawal from social activities.

I like this expansive version of what depression is because depression affects more than just your mood and maybe you're thinking like *"Well I'm sad, but I don't think I'm depressed."* However, you also can't get out of bed, and you've stopped going out with friends. I want us to have a clear idea of what depression can look like so that we have all the knowledge we need to overcome depression. Interestingly enough depression is the last stage before acceptance which is the final stage of grief. As I said earlier, I do honestly believe it is the hardest stage to overcome because it takes a lot to get yourself back to the "normal" you probably felt before losing that child, that mother, that father, or that sibling. I want to take some time and really hammer out all the ins and outs of what I know to be true about depression, what God has revealed to me, and how God is available to you even in the most broken place of this grief.

Depression, unlike sadness, has a way of changing you. In any stage of grief, if you stay there long enough you risk losing yourself. With depression, it's easy to give into the withdrawal and retreat from family and friends. It's easy to become a shell of your former self. Something I used to do a lot when I was experiencing depression was disassociating. Disassociating is when you intentionally try to disconnect yourself from negative feelings or thoughts associated with trauma.

I had to continue to show up for my family and that meant shutting down a lot of the time. Disassociating is a defense mechanism and it is not advised or what we would deem a normal way of coping. Sometime after my nervous breakdown when the depression manifested, and it got harder to keep the pain out, disassociating is what started to take place. I would be in a room full of family and friends and they would start to talk about my mom, or sometimes I would just have random thoughts of her and I would have to try to separate myself from the feelings that tried to come. I would bite the inside of my cheeks and push the emotions back down and focus my attention on something new. By something new, this would usually be the precursor to me going to grab a bottle. *"Let's drink"* I'd say or see if anyone wanted to go out to the bar. It wasn't until the nighttime, when I was alone that I couldn't sleep, that the depression, the feelings I spent all day chasing away would come.

I'd just lay there wishing I could run away, without telling anyone. The depression made me feel as though I was alone fighting something that no one would even understand anyway, so why would anyone care if I disappeared? I had already gotten over the wanting to die part, remember I was still filled with the fear that I was going to die anyway. Disappearing wasn't quite like dying.

It meant that I could go and feel the feels and not be responsible for anyone or anything and I could drink, sleep with whoever, and smoke as much as I wanted until the sadness just left me. I would lay there planning out how I would do it.

First, I would have to map out exactly how many paychecks I needed to save up in order to stay away long enough. I would consider places I could go that I may also be able to start a new job if needed. I would think about the letter I would write to my family and friends, letting them know that I was okay, and that I would reach out when I could.

Can I tell you something about depression? You can't run from it. I tried to relocate with my depression still in tow. I thought that getting away and never looking back would solve everything. Every part of my life at that point felt broken, felt wrong. Of course, I thought running away and starting a new life would fix the God sized hole in my heart. I mentioned I was over the wanting to die part, but maybe you aren't. When I was in high school and throughout most of college I wanted to die.

I would fantasize about running my car off the road or stepping out into the street or getting kidnapped and killed. I thought that death was the only way to escape the pain that I was feeling.

Maybe you think death is the only way to stop the pain you're stuck in, and even better you'll get to be with your loved one. Listen, death doesn't really end the problem. It only seems that way because it's so final. But if you die, without Christ in your life you may not end up in heaven with your loved one. More than that, you'll leave people here to feel the same feelings we've been talking about in this entire book. If you killed yourself the only person that would benefit from that seems like it would be you, but it would actually be no one. God has a tremendous plan for your life, even if right now it doesn't seem that way, even if right now all you see is darkness.

I want you to think about at least three people or even just one person whose life would be just as altered, if not more than yours was, if you died.

One night in my early depression days, before my mom passed away, I would get a bottle of pills and I was fully prepared to die. I was so exhausted. I felt alone. I felt like a burden. I felt empty. I was sitting there already crying into my pillow and I started to think about my family. I started to think about how my cousin would feel if she opened the bedroom door to my body, or worse if her children did. I started to think about the life they would be left with.

I shoved the pills back into the bottle and I called for help. I called a suicide hotline and they sent someone to my house to take me to a crisis center.

You're not alone and while overcoming depression may not be an overnight thing, you have a Father in heaven who is concerned about you. You have friends and family who are concerned about you. Maybe you're saying, I don't have any friends or family. There's a suicide hotline, or warm line that you can call with people on the other end that care about

YOU! Death can carry such a heavy burden but let God help you carry the load. Submit the depression to Him.

Understanding Depression

Again, King David, was described as a man after God's own heart. King David experienced moments of depression and in the book of Psalms, you can sense that they were written by someone deep in sorrow. This gives biblical indication that this life is not without its sorrows.

Maybe you can relate.

"O Lord, how long will you forget me? Forever? How long will you look the other way? How long must I struggle with anguish in my soul, with sorrow in my heart every day? How long will my enemy have the upper hand? Turn and answer me, O Lord my God! Restore the sparkle to my eyes, or I will die. Don't let my enemies gloat, saying, "We have defeated him!" Don't let them rejoice at my downfall." Psalms 13:1-4 NLT

"I am worn out from sobbing. All night I flood my bed with weeping, drenching it with my tears. My vision is blurred by grief; my eyes are worn out because of all my enemies." Psalms 6:6-7 NLT

"God, my God! Why would you abandon me now? Why do you remain distant, refusing to answer my tearful cries in the day and my desperate cries for your help in the night? I can't stop sobbing. Where are you, my God?" Psalms 22:1-2 TPT

David was clearly experiencing moments of sorrow, grief, and depression through his life. There were times where David thought God abandoned him. David felt alone, he says to God, don't you hear my cries? I can definitely remember the sleepless nights where my tears soaked my bed and I wondered where God was. King David is someone who pursued the heart of God and still encountered grief and depression in His life.

Maybe, you're falling into the depression stage of your loss. What might that look like:

Characteristics of Depression:

- Feeling sad, empty, or numb.
- Feeling overwhelmed by the daily things you have to do.
- Experiencing hopelessness.
- Thinking that no one will understand what you're going through.
- Crying often.
- Isolating or withdrawing from others.
- Sleeping or staying in bed all day.

All of these things in a different context may seem normal. However, there may be extremes. If you are experiencing a set of these characteristics and they overwhelm you to the point that you're disregarding daily tasks, then this is when I would suggest that you're likely experiencing the depression stage of grief.

The good news is that Jesus made a way for us to overcome depression. He defeated depression when He went to the cross for you. So, I want you to let go of the idea that it's too much for you to overcome.

Overcoming Depression

Earlier we looked at several scriptures in the book of psalms that pointed to King David experiencing depression. Let's see the biblical ways to overcome depression by looking at each of these psalms.

"Go away, all you who do evil, for the Lord has heard my weeping. The Lord has heard my plea; the Lord will answer my prayer." Psalm 6:8-9 NLT

David just a verse up was complaining of how deep his grief and sorrow was. David said that his tears filled his bed. In just another verse over David places his assurance in his God. The Lord has heard my weeping, he proclaims. How did David know that the Lord had heard his weeping and that the Lord would answer his prayer? If you read more into David's story, you will find out that the Lord was always faithful to David, even during his grief. In 2 Samuel, God makes a promise to David that He would establish David's kingdom and lineage forever.

"Now go and say to my servant David, 'This is what the Lord of Heaven's Armies has declared: I took you from tending sheep in the pasture and selected you to be the leader of my people Israel. I have been with you wherever you have gone, and I have destroyed all your enemies before your eyes. Now I will make your name as famous as anyone who has ever lived on the earth!" 2 Samuel 7:8-9 NLT

We even see in the verse that the Lord had reminded David that He has been with him wherever he had gone, making a way for him. David was able to declare that the Lord had heard him in his sorrows because he knew that part of God's character is that He is faithful, and that God would be there no matter what emotion David faced.

The Bible is filled with promises of God's faithfulness to His people, and even to you. So, here's the first step to overcoming depression:

1. Remember God is with you and recall His faithfulness.

"And the Lord, He is the One who goes before you. He will be with you; He will not leave you nor forsake you; do not fear nor be dismayed." Deuteronomy 31:8 NKJV

"But now, thus says the Lord, who created you, O Jacob, And He who formed you, O Israel: "Fear not, for I have redeemed you; I have called you by your name; You are Mine. When you pass through the waters, I will be with you; And through the rivers, they shall not overflow you. When you walk through the fire, you shall not be burned, Nor shall the flame scorch you." Isaiah 43:1-2 NKJV

"Even when your path takes me through the valley of deepest darkness, fear will never conquer me, for you already have! Your authority is my strength and my peace. The comfort of your love takes away my fear. I'll never be lonely, for you are near." Psalm 23:4 TPT

God's word assures us that even when we go through the deepest darkness, He is there. Depression may feel like it is a depth is a place of no return, but in this you must remind yourself that God is with you. You must recall the promises of God. If you convince yourself in the sadness that God is not there it only becomes darker. God is the light that breaks through every bit of darkness, no matter how deep. The lie of depression that you are alone works as a barrier between you and God.

Imagine a door that leads to the outside. Let's say your own front door. How would you know that beyond that door, it actually leads to outside?

Well, because the door is always there. For your entire life, every time you open the front door, the outside is there including the grass, the trees, the sun, the porch, and whatever else is on the other side of your front door. You don't have to guess what's on the other side of that door, you just know. Now let's say that outside, the light from the sun, the beautiful blue sky, represents God. What's the barrier between you and the outside? The door.

The reason that depression uses a demonic door that is represented by the lie that you're alone, is so that you never open it and realize what your heart already knows is on the other side. Instead of seeing God for who He is and where He is, there's this big lie, that He isn't there, when really He's just on the other side, closer than that He's right there. I don't know about your front door but mine isn't that thick you can probably very easily break through it with the right tools. Recalling what the word of God says in your depression, declaring what the word of God says when you feel alone is the tool that is going to tear down every bit of this feeling and reveal to you that your father has always been there.

The next way that we overcome depression is found in our next scripture.

"I have always trusted in your kindness, so answer me. I will spin in a circle of joy when your salvation lifts me up. I will sing my song of joy to you, Yahweh, for in all of this you have strengthened my soul. My enemies say that I have no Savior, but I know that I have one in you!" Psalms 13:5-6 TPT

What I love about the way the passion translation has presented this scripture is that David says, *"I will spin in a circle of joy when your salvation lifts me up. I will sing my song of joy to you."* He goes on to say how the Lord has strengthened his soul. Can I submit to you that the way out of this depression is in your song of joy to the Lord. It's in your praise!

2. Put on a garment of praise!

Many times, we read of King David singing praises to the Lord in his sorrow. He was a true worshiper and understood that when he praised, it was a reminder to his soul of the goodness of God, which also gave him strength.

Earlier, we referenced Psalms 42 where David commanded his soul to praise the Lord. It is very hard to praise God for His goodness and also be sad. When we praise God it begins to lift the heaviness!

Here's the next scripture:

"*The Spirit of the Lord God is upon Me, Because the Lord has anointed Me To preach good tidings to the poor; He has sent Me to heal the brokenhearted, To proclaim liberty to the captives, And the opening of the prison to those who are bound; To proclaim the acceptable year of the Lord, And the day of vengeance of our God; To comfort all who mourn, To console those who mourn in Zion, To give them beauty for ashes, The oil of joy for mourning, The garment of praise for the spirit of heaviness; That they may be called trees of righteousness, The planting of the Lord, that He may be glorified.*" Isaiah 61:1-3 NKJV

For context, the book of Isaiah is a book that prophesies the coming of the Messiah. This particular verse is also highlighting the role of our Savior. We can see that our Savior has come to heal the brokenhearted, to make free those who are bound, to comfort all who mourn, to give beauty for ashes, and to give the oil of joy for mourning. If this scripture doesn't point to the fact that Jesus quite literally has a solution for every facet of grief, then I don't know what does. He is ready to heal the brokenness that you feel from the loss and to set you free from the bondage of depression.

So, in this depression, a hard stage of grief, here is another promise of God, He will comfort you. He promises a garment of praise for your heaviness.

A garment is an article of clothing, something that you put on. So, the Lord says He gives you something to put on when you are feeling heavy, weighed down, depressed, and that's your praise. When it's cold outside, you put on a coat, so when you're falling into these feelings of depression, put on your praise. How do you put on praise? The Bible says in Psalm 100 to "*make a joyful noise to the Lord, to come before Him with singing, to enter His gates with thanksgiving.*"

The Hebrew word for praise is Tehilla which translates to a song of praise. This is a song of adoration. You put on praise by singing a song of love and adoration to the Lord. You might be thinking how can I sing of love to Him in this dark place? Command your soul.

My first experience with God was at an old school Pentecostal, bible believing, tambourine shaking, Holy Ghost filled church. Sometimes I would hear the older saints keep a praise on their lips. Like singing the old hymn, "*I need Thee. Oooh, I need Thee. Every hour I need Thee. Oh, bless me now, my Savior. I come to Thee.*

Of course, at that time I couldn't see the importance of it. I would just wonder why they would sing these old songs all the time. I believe it was because they understood the importance of keeping praise in their mouth so that their mind, will, and emotions would follow.

I didn't know a lot of gospel songs by heart when I first started living the life of a Christian, but when I would miss my mom I would sing Amazing grace. I'm sure it doesn't sound like much but eventually I learned my own songs of praise. I learned to sing to the Lord of how good He was, I started to sing of His beauty, and how He was the only one who could make me whole. The amazing thing about it is that it takes my focus away from the sorrows and the trials of the day and encourages me. When you're going through depression, keep going, don't stay there, sing a song of praise to Him, encourage yourself in the Lord.

Psalm 100:2 says to *come before Him with praise*, but other versions say to sing your way into His presence. I want to encourage you to start to sing your way into His presence. He's waiting.

Practical ways to overcome depression:

1. ***Allow others to be there for you.***
   - Depression creates a desire to want to isolate, so make intentional steps to do the opposite.
   - Call some friends over. It may be hard to talk, but allow them to be there for you, even if that means sitting there quietly while you all watch a movie.

2. ***Spend time at church surrounded by other believers who will keep you encouraged.***
   - This is a different kind of support and it will provide you will an outlet with viable feedback and coping skills for what you are experiencing.
   - I want to also encourage you in this step to find a Christian counselor, or see if your church offers short term counseling, or grief classes. I say this because it's going to be important that the information and feedback you are getting is Godly advice that will help you overcome.

3. ***Don't suppress your feelings.***
    - This has been a common theme throughout this book because pushing your feelings aside is unrealistic and potentially hazardous. What I mean by this is, usually the way one suppresses their emotions is by way of disassociating or medicating and neither of those things will solve the problem. Instead, it will provide only a temporary band aid.
    - Journal about the way you are feeling on a regular basis. Practice freewriting. Don't stop to think about what you want to say or what sounds good, just write. Dump all your feelings for that time onto a page and out of your heart, and it's okay to cry.
    - Crying is cathartic, meaning it's an emotional release. Don't hide your tears. When Lazarus died, even Jesus cried. *"Then tears streamed down Jesus' face."* John 11:35 TPT

4. ***Find a praise song or songs that encourage you.***
    - We talked a lot about praise being our weapon and our way out, now it's time to put it into practice. Find praise songs that encourage, create a playlist, and sing along. Eventually your heart will create its own song as God heals you.

5. ***Remember that healing takes time.***
    - Give yourself space to go through the pain but go through! Don't wallow in it and don't stay there.
    - When you feel yourself getting stuck, go back to the first step. Let people be there for you.

Here are the scriptures I want you to meditate on as you make your way out of depression:

"You keep track of all my sorrows. You have collected all my tears in your bottle. You have recorded each one in your book." Psalm 56:8 NLT **(Remember it's okay to cry. God is literally right there with you, watching over your sorrows, and ready to heal your broken heart.)**

"Fear not, for I am with you; Be not dismayed, for I am your God. I will strengthen you, Yes, I will help you, I will uphold you with My righteous right hand." Isaiah 41:10 NKJV

"All praise to God, the Father of our Lord Jesus Christ. God is our merciful Father and the source of all comfort. He comforts us in all our troubles so that we can comfort others. When they are troubled, we will be able to give them the same comfort God has given us." 2 Corinthians 1:3-4 NLT

Let's Pray

Lord, I thank You that there is no place in the world that You would rather be, than with Your son or daughter as they experience the pain of this loss. I thank You that you are in position ready to catch every tear and bring healing to even the emptiest place in their heart. I ask that You cover them in Your love that comforts beyond what we can imagine. I ask that they begin to trust You and to bring their sorrows to You instead of isolating or turning to the comforts of the world that only provide temporary pleasure. I thank You Father that You love them more than anything and have a divine plan to see them through to the other side of this depression. I bind all depression in Your name and speak healing to every wound left behind by this loss.

In Jesus name, Amen

6

Acceptance

All things considered; I have learned that grief takes time. Losing my mom happened fast, but the process of grief, no matter how familiar I became with each stage took time. Grief is and will always be a process of going though, not getting over.

When we look at loss from the perspective of death, loss of a job, loss of a friendship, or even loss of time, we don't ever just get over it. In fact, something I've found is that getting over it doesn't actually work because you never actually went through anything. Getting over it almost implies that you're required to dismiss the trauma and forget that it ever happened.

In the beginning of my grief process that's exactly what I was doing, I was dismissing it, I was compartmentalizing the trauma, and I was moving forward to the next part of living. Don't get me wrong, I did have to learn to live without my mom but I couldn't truly do that until I processed through the loss.

As we venture into this last and most powerful stage, acceptance, I want to give you a glimpse at my grief timeline.

My mom passed away in 2016. However, I don't think I hit the acceptance stage of this loss until 2022. Six years. It took me six years to reach the stage where I learned to live without my mom. Granted the first three years I was angry, and sad, and drunk, and getting OVER it. It wasn't until I started inviting God back into my life that I started to go THROUGH it.

Everything that you've read up until this point, every stage I allowed God to take me through, took time. I know it might seem scary or daunting to think that you don't have six years to go through what you're feeling now. No matter what type of loss you may be experiencing, you're here. God led you to this book, because He cares about your loss more than anyone, and wants to help you through it no matter the time.

The good thing about it is, God is a redeemer of time, so however long it takes to walk through this loss with Him, it is never time wasted. I think the ugly scary part would be if it had taken me six years and I was still in denial, and still shutting the trauma down. I share that because I would not be going through it, I would still be nursing the pain with alcohol, and that to me sounds like time wasted.

For us to assess the difference between when I stopped going through all those stages to coming to a place of acceptance we need to look at the definition of acceptance.

The APA dictionary of psychology describes the acceptance stage of grief as some degree of emotional detachment, objectivity, or resignation on the part of oneself or an important other to the reality of impending or actual death, other great loss, or trauma. What this means is simply that you have come to a place where we accept and understand the reality of the loss, you are able to look forward to the future knowing what happened.

Let's break that definition down. The first line says that there will be some degree of emotional detachment. Before my mom passed she would talk about her mom's death a lot. For the first few months after my grandma passed my mom would break into tears at the most random moments, she walked around very broken for a long time.

In the beginning of a loss, we are extremely emotionally invested in the way the loss has made us feel. When I was in the thick of my grief, if I wasn't carefully minding my feelings anything could make me cry.

I was driving on the way to school one morning, "Don't Know Why", by Nora Jones came on, and I remembered that my mom used to always put it on repeat. I guess I forgot it was in my playlist and this was the first time I was hearing it since she died. I burst into tears and I spent the entire day playing that song over and over until I found myself buried in a bottle on my bedroom floor.

When we move into the acceptance stage of grief it's not to say that there won't be a mother's day that you'll see a mother and daughter deep in embrace and that won't break your heart, because it will. The reminder of loss sometimes still hurts, even though we have accepted that it's gone. That's why even after you've gone through a bad breakup and accepted that it's over, you can walk past someone wearing that exact cologne or perfume that your ex used to wear and your heart winces just a little. The thing is, hearing Norah Jones makes me miss my mommy and it always will, but do I spend the day crying at the sound of Norah's voice in my car, no. I spend that moment remembering how much I loved her and how much I miss her, and then the next song comes on, and the moment passes.

As you begin to accept the loss, you will no longer be emotionally pulled by it. It won't dictate your days, weeks, and months anymore.

Accepting loss, especially that of someone you love, looks a lot like remembering the beauty of a butterfly that lingered in your presence and flew away. You pause, you look, you smile, you feel the beauty of what that moment has to offer, and then you keep going. Accepting the loss of a loved one is like dandelions in the wind. Do you remember when you were a kid running around in a field of grass with friends and you stumbled upon a dandelion?

You would pick it up and with deep seated curiosity you would admire its beauty. But we all knew the same thing, and that is, we would blow and watch the seeds of the dandelion be carried off by the wind. Even if you didn't realize it, for a moment you would have to accept knowing that it was gone, but you'd laugh and continue running, with a heart filled with joy.

Loss is an extremely difficult but natural part of life. We get the privilege of experiencing and admiring the beauty and comfort of knowing someone, until they are carried away in the wind, living on in our memories.

That's just it, they live in a place where no one can uproot the experience you had from knowing them. I got to love my mom for 25 years of my life, it doesn't seem like long enough, and it wasn't.

But I remember that when I was afraid she would climb into bed with me as a kid, or I could climb into her bed at 19 and lay there without saying anything, and she just knew. I get to remember that she had the loudest, craziest, most contagious laugh on the planet, and that I would imitate her voice just to get her to laugh. I get to remember that she loved me and my siblings more than life itself and that she would go to war over us. It was a deep honor and privilege to have her in my life for as long as I did and, like that precious moment with that dandelion, there came a time where I learned to live without her.

I'd be lying if I said I didn't cry through most of this book, but it's because I get to recall the one person in the world that I never thought I could live without. I think about how bizarre it is that I fully surrendered my life to Jesus and through that I've gone on mission trips around the world, and I often wonder what my mom would say.

What if I stayed in the bottom of that bottle?

What if you stay where you are?

What beautiful and amazing and wonderful thing are you missing out on that God wants to do in your life?

Acceptance will never mean forgetting and that you won't cry, or that your life will look the same. Acceptance means you learn to live a full life remembering the beauty of a moment. Your family needs you; your children need you; your husband or wife, they need you. Believe it or not, this life that you're living amongst the people that love you, this is their moment. Don't slip away before God has called you.

Do me a favor, in a moment I'm going to ask you to close your eyes and I want you to picture yourself as a kid, laughing, excited, not yet touched by the cares of the world. See yourself in this massive field of dandelions, the sun is shining brightly on your face. Now close your eyes and take a big deep breath. In this breath I want you to remember your loss, I want you to pull in the pain, the fear, the uneasy feeling of doing life without them.

Now blow. Watch the seeds float away in the wind as you give God the depression, and you surrender the pain, as you release the not knowing.

When you've come up from experiencing this moment, feel free to sit the book down and let the Holy Spirit work in this moment. But when you come up I want you to remember that in that moment when you blew away the seeds, God was there.

He is in the air that brushes past your cheek. He's in the sun that's shining on your smile, and your tears. He's in the sound of the wind. You were never alone in this. God was in the house that night I got that phone call. He was in the car ride to the hospital. He was in the room as my mom took her last breath and He's here now as you feel that weight being lifted off your chest. Breathe.

Walking in Acceptance

I want us to look at this also from a practical standpoint as well. So, let's look at some characteristics of the acceptance stage:

- Feeling positive and hopeful.
- Being able to tolerate emotions and be vulnerable.
- Engaging in your new reality, instead of dwelling on what you thought it would be.
- Feeling more secure and relaxed.
- Being more present.
- Taking care of yourself.

All of these things will be a product of you learning to live with the loss you have experienced. As you move forward, your joy should increase. You should start to experience hope for what is to come. It is okay to make plans for what is next without diminishing the importance of the loss. Emotions will come and go but in this stage they should no longer be consuming you, this is the part where you start to learn to go to God with your emotions. Realistically there may be days where it's very hard, but you will need to develop a habit of going to God in those hard times.

"So, here's what I've learned through it all: Leave all your cares and anxieties at the feet of the Lord, and measureless grace will strengthen you." Psalms 55:22 TPT

The one thing that I want you to take away from this entire process is that God is with you. Of course, we need our friends and our family, sometimes we even need to see professional counselors, but nobody will be able to sustain you the way that the Lord will. He's going to be your life raft through all of this, and honestly for the rest of your life.

As I started to accept my loss, the fog started to lift. I stopped disassociating so much and started praying.

I started allowing myself to feel. I remained in therapy with a Christian therapist. It truly changed my life to be able to have a safe place each week to talk through what I was feeling in a therapeutic and productive manner, so I am a huge advocate for therapy. God gave us therapy to help you out, but that's including Him.

Here are some practical ways to walk in acceptance:

1. ***Plan for the future.***
   - Part of feeling hopeful of what's to come, is having dreams. I want you to create a list of things that you have either put off doing or that you desire to do.
   - Now take the most important thing on that list and create some action steps. What steps are you going to take to achieve this goal? Then begin working towards it.

2. ***Start spending more time with those you love.***
   - No more isolating. It's time to create moments that will last a lifetime with the people that you love. Reach out to people you may have pushed away during this time of grief, make amends, and remember that you love each other.

3. ***Seek professional help.***
   - It's okay if you need to be in therapy through all of this.
   - Talk to your medical insurance provider, see what mental health resources are available to you.

4. ***Give yourself some time.***
   - Be kind to yourself in all of this and remember grief is a process. It's okay to have bad days.
   - Do something nice for yourself on the days you feel stronger by taking yourself to a movie, purchase that item you've been looking at for weeks, or spend the day with someone you love.

The scriptures I want you to meditate on as we close this final stage are those that remind us of God's goodness and what joy we WILL have in Him:

"You will show me the way of life, granting me the joy of your presence and the pleasures of living with you forever." Psalms 16:11 NLT

"Go and enjoy choice food and sweet drinks and send some to those who have nothing prepared. This day is holy to our Lord. Do not grieve, for the joy of the Lord is your strength." Nehemiah 8:10 NIV

"The Lord is good, a refuge in times of trouble. He cares for those who trust in him." Nahum 1:7 NIV

"For the Lord is good and his love endures forever; his faithfulness continues through all generations." Psalms 100:5 NIV

Let's Pray.

Lord, I thank You for the reader of this book and that you have stood by their side through this season of grief and loss. As they pass over into the acceptance of this loss, they begin to teach them how to live without the person or thing that they dearly loved. I thank You for the memories left behind of goodness and joy. I pray that they will be fulfilled by remembering, but not bound. Fill them with a deeper level of compassion for themselves as they learn a new way of life. Give them infectious laughter, beautiful dreams, and hope for the future. Strengthen them in your joy.

In Jesus name, Amen.

7

Hope

There is no RIGHT WAY to grieve. I wish that there was an exact science to it. Even with all the research and resources that we have, there is no way someone can tell you how to grieve. This book is not intended to tell you how to grieve, but rather, it was written to be a light shining in the darkness, one that reminds you that there's life worth living after loss.

If you feel like you are ill equipped to handle this loss, that's ok. Remember that seeking professional help is an option. I am going to share resources for California, along with national lines. However, no matter what state you live in, there will also be resources for when you feel overwhelmed, such as peer support lines or warm lines.

Asking for help doesn't always mean your need is as extreme as wanting to end your life, but it can mean you need an extra hand to help you come out on the other end of this, successfully. When I went to the crisis rehabilitation center it was my profound cry for help. It was a huge blessing in my life because I could not get it together on my own, and it's not even to say that I was on the verge of ending my life, but I was losing myself in my grief and depression.

For 30 days I was surrounded by a professional support team that guided me out of it. This is not to say that God was not there, and it doesn't replace the fact that you need to put God first. However, I couldn't see God through the waves that kept crashing over me.

Maybe, you do need help. This is what I want you to do. Call a friend or a family member that you trust with your heart. Tell them what's going on and be vulnerable about needing help. Admitting you need help is the first step and sometimes it's easier with the people closest to us that love us, the ones that won't judge you.

For me, it was my cousin/best friend. She has been one of the closest people to me since I was 9 years old. So, it was easy to tell her that I was reaching my breaking point. This person should be someone that will come by your side when you're in distress. No one can be there 24/7, which is why we have God. However, when I called, when I needed her, she was there. No judgement, just love.

And still maybe, you just need to reconnect with God. I had that realization too. So, I want to encourage you to give God your time, starting now. Pick a time each day that you're going to spend with Him, unfolding these feelings.

This doesn't have to start off as hours and hours, it can be thirty minutes a day to simply reconnect with Him. Get in a Holy spirit filled, Bible believing church and immerse yourself there. Surround yourself with a community of Godly prayer warriors and intercessors who know how to go to the Father on your behalf.

There is more than just acceptance of losing something or someone that you love. There is hope. I want you to know that I am praying for you. I want you to know that my mom's death was not in vain. I know that my mom's death carried a purpose that gets to live on through me. I want you to know that God gave me this insight into grief so that you wouldn't stay where you are. You were made to be somebody that overcomes and I'm rooting for you.

"Then God's wonderful peace that transcends human understanding, will guard your heart and mind through Jesus Christ. Philippians 4:7 TPT

MENTAL HEALTH RESOURCES

1. NAMI - National Alliance on Mental Health
   - 1-800-950-NAMI (6264) OR text "Helpline" to 62640
   - Email: **helpline@nami.org**
2. National Suicide Prevention
   - 1-800-273-8255 (TALK) or 988
3. Cal Hope Warm Line
   - Call or Text (833) 317-HOPE (4673)
4. NAMI- Warm line directly website
   - **www.nami.org**, search warm line directory

These are just a few resources available nationally and in California. If you need help, you can also google resources in your state or location as well.

ACKNOWLEDGMENTS

I want to first thank **God** for the love and compassion He has shown not only in my life, but even as I wrote this book. It is through His loving kindness through my season of grief that He revealed Himself to me, and my life will never be the same.

I give my heartfelt thanks and appreciation to my mentor **Julia Thronson** who stewarded a large portion of my growth and continues to believe in every endeavor the Lord planted in me.

Thank you to my **family** who stood together when we lost my mom and remained a steady support system through the grief.

Thank you to **Ronnekka Spears**, my best friend who remained by my side through every single stage of grief and only had love and empathy to offer in whatever capacity I needed.

To **Fernanda Villa**, thank you for being a constant support in my walk with Christ and for writing the forward address to this book. Forever, praying for you and thanking God for you.

I want to express thanks to my **friends** who make it possible for me to have the courage to step out in faith and write this book.

I want to give a heartfelt thanks to my publisher, **Pastor Michelle Collins**, who coached me and walked me through the process of writing my first book. I am grateful for the mentorship and ministry that was sown into this book.

ABOUT THE AUTHOR

Nichelle Lawrence is an author and advocate for healing through faith, drawing on her own experience of trauma. With a degree in Psychology and a background in mental health, she has walked alongside many on their journey to emotional and spiritual restoration, offering tools for true freedom in Christ.

Born in Los Angeles, California, Nichelle's life has been a testament to the transformative power of God. Her personal story of overcoming trauma through surrender to Christ, serves as the foundation of her work.

In her debut book, *Unending Grace*, Nichelle shares a message of hope, equipping readers with biblical wisdom and practical tools for those navigating loss. Her words encourage others to embrace healing, trust in God's faithfulness, and discover grace on the other side of grief.

Made in the USA
Las Vegas, NV
08 December 2025

35977689R00059